A Pan-Asian Cookbook

Unlock the Secrets of Asian Cuisine with these Easy-to-Make Recipes!

by

Josephine Ellise

Copyright Notices

Table of Contents

Introduction

Would you fancy relishing taste and health together?

It is rare that one finds a combination of taste and healthiness. These Pan-Asian dishes include ingredients that are high in nutrients such as vitamins and minerals. And then there's the fact that Pan-Asian cuisine uses methods of preparation that allow these healthy elements to stay put during cooking.

"A Pan-Asian Cookbook" is a synthesis of culinary traditions from the world's largest continent. To gain access to authentic, time-tested recipes representing various flavor profiles across Asia.

Delving deeper into regions based upon geographical grouping, the primary divisions consist of East, South, West, or Central zones. The Western segment encompasses the savory delights originating from the Middle Eastern vicinity while the heartland focuses on distinctive dishes from locations like Turkey, Kazakhstan, Iran, Israel and Uzbekistan among others. Cuisines of southern Asia represent an insanely great diversity of flavors, spices and ideas. From India to Pakistan, Bangladesh to Sri Lanka, these neighboring countries are innovating in the kitchen and putting a dent in the universe with their bold, memorable dishes. It's also often referred to as "Desi" food.

Discover a world of taste sensations with the diverse culinary traditions of East Asia. Embrace the diverse range of dishes and cooking methods that come from five fascinating nations: China, Mongolia, South Korea, Japan and Taiwan, all brimming with mouthwatering flavors waiting to be uncovered. Easy-to-prepare Oriental cuisine features exciting dishes that will leave everyone impressed.

Unlock the wonders of East Asia without breaking a sweat by trying out the effortless steps provided in this book. It comprises a combination of noodles, salmon and beef mix, Asian BBQ chicken and egg soup etc.

Craving delectable yet healthy grub? Fret not! Embark on a journey through a delightful array of mouthwatering Asian dishes that promise both flavor and wellbeing.

By incorporating zesty seasonings and fragrant spices, each dish guarantees to captivate your senses. Plus, many Asian soups boast impressive nutrient contents that enhance the overall meal experience. Experiment with unique combinations to create your perfect Asian feasts every week! Let's get started!

vvvvvvvvvvvvvvvvvvvvvvvvvvvvvv

1. Salmon & Cabbage Stir-Fry

Salmon & cabbage stir-fry dish is a perfect dinner dish with lots of flavors and charm. It's the best romantic dinner recipe to enjoy with your loved ones. A bowl full of spices with salmon and cabbage makes it a perfect blend of taste and texture.

Serve: 2-4

Prep Time: 30 minutes

List of Ingredients:

- 1 pack of mushroom
- 2 tablespoons of miso
- 1 tablespoon of soy sauce
- 1 tablespoon of mirin
- 1/2 teaspoon of white sugar
- Sesame seeds, roasted
- 7 oz of boneless salmon
- 1 small wedge of cabbage
- 2 tablespoons of unsalted butter
- 1 tablespoon of cornstarch
- Salt, to taste

vvvvvvvvvvvvvvvvvvvvvvvvvvvvvvvv

Method:

I. Prepare the ingredients: Begin by cutting the salmon into bite-sized pieces. In a bowl, coat the salmon with salt and cornstarch, ensuring each piece is well coated.

II. Heat the pan: Place the pan over medium-high heat and add oil. Once the oil is hot, add unsalted butter and a pinch of salt.

III. Stir-fry the salmon: Add the coated salmon pieces to the pan and stir-fry them until they are cooked through and lightly browned on the outside.

IV. Add the vegetables: Transfer the cabbage and mushrooms to the pan with the cooked salmon.

V. Prepare the sauce: In a small bowl, mix together miso, soy sauce, mirin, and sugar until well combined.

VI. Pour the sauce: Pour the prepared sauce over the salmon, cabbage, and mushrooms in the pan. Stir everything together to evenly distribute the sauce.

VII. Cook and blend: Continue cooking and stirring the ingredients until the cabbage is slightly wilted and tender, and the flavors have melded together.

VIII. Garnish and serve: Sprinkle the stir-fry with sesame seeds for an added touch of flavor and visual appeal. Serve the Salmon and Cabbage Stir-Fry hot.

Cooking notes:

I. Adjust the amount of salt and seasoning according to your taste preferences.

II. Be careful not to overcook the salmon, as it can become dry. Aim for a tender and slightly flaky texture.

III. Feel free to add other vegetables of your choice, such as bell peppers or carrots, to enhance the nutritional value and add more variety to the stir-fry.

IV. Serve the dish with steamed rice or noodles for a complete and satisfying meal.

V. Enjoy the delicious flavors and healthy combination of salmon and cabbage in this flavorful stir-fry!

2. Asian BBQ Chicken

Asian BBQ chicken is a tasteful and delicious chicken dish for dinner. It's spicy, hot, and worth your taste buds. A perfect chicken dinner can be served with fried rice. Also, it has an oven effect color on the chicken that makes it look authentic and colorful.

Serve: 4

Prep Time: 1 hour 15 minutes

List of Ingredients:

- 2 tablespoons of char siu sauce
- 1 teaspoon of rice vinegar
- 1 teaspoon of red chili paste (optional)
- To taste: salt & pepper
- 2 chicken breasts
- 1 tablespoon of garlic & ginger
- 1 teaspoon of honey
- 1/2 teaspoon of sesame oil

vvvvvvvvvvvvvvvvvvvvvvvvvvvvvvv

Method:

I. Prepare the marinade: In a bowl, combine garlic, ginger, honey, red chili sauce, rice vinegar, red chili paste, sesame oil, salt, pepper, and char siu sauce. Mix well to create the marinade.

II. Marinate the chicken: Add chicken breasts to the marinade, ensuring they are fully coated. Allow the chicken to marinate for at least 20 minutes, allowing the flavors to infuse.

III. Heat the pan: Place a pan over medium heat and add a small amount of oil to prevent sticking.

IV. Cook the chicken: Place the marinated chicken breasts in the heated pan and cook for 15-20 minutes, flipping occasionally, until the chicken is cooked through and nicely browned on both sides.

V. Check for doneness: Ensure the chicken reaches an internal temperature of 165°F (74°C) using a meat thermometer to ensure it is cooked thoroughly.

VI. Rest the chicken: Once cooked, remove the chicken from the pan and let it rest for a few minutes to allow the juices to redistribute and the flavors to settle.

VII. Serve hot: Slice the Asian BBQ chicken and serve it hot, allowing the juicy and flavorful chicken to be the star of the dish.

VIII. Enjoy the flavors: Savor the succulent and aromatic Asian BBQ chicken with your favorite side dishes or as part of a rice or noodle bowl.

Cooking notes:

I. You can adjust the amount of chili sauce and chili paste according to your preferred level of spiciness.

II. For extra tenderness, consider marinating the chicken for a longer period, such as overnight in the refrigerator.

III. Char siu sauce can be found in Asian grocery stores or you can make your own by combining hoisin sauce, honey, soy sauce, and Chinese five-spice powder.

IV. To add a beautiful charred appearance, you can grill the marinated chicken instead of pan-cooking it.

V. Garnish the dish with sliced green onions and sesame seeds for added flavor and visual appeal.

VI. Enjoy the mouthwatering flavors of your homemade Asian BBQ chicken!

3. Chili Chicken

Chili chicken is the most popular Indo-Chinese dish served as a starter for your dinner. It's tangy, spicy, and with lots of amazing flavors of garlic, ginger, eggs, green chilies, and soy sauce.

Serve: 2

Prep Time: 55 Minutes

List of Ingredients:

- 1 egg
- 1/2 teaspoon of garlic paste
- 1 tablespoon of salt
- Oil, for deep fry
- 2 teaspoons of green chilies, sliced
- 1 tablespoon of soy sauce
- Green chilies, for garnishing
- 12 oz of boneless chicken, diced
- 1/2 cup of corn flour
- 1/2 teaspoon of ginger paste
- 2 cups of onions, sliced
- 2 tablespoons of vinegar

vvvvvvvvvvvvvvvvvvvvvvvvvvvv

Method:

I. Prepare the batter: In a bowl, combine eggs, corn flour, ginger and garlic paste. Add some water to achieve a smooth consistency. Marinate the chicken pieces in this batter, ensuring they are well coated. Set it aside for 30 minutes to marinate.

II. Heat oil for frying: In a wok or deep frying pan, heat oil for deep frying the chicken pieces until it reaches the desired temperature.

III. Fry the chicken: Carefully place the marinated chicken pieces in the hot oil and deep fry them until they are golden brown and cooked through. Use a slotted spoon to remove the chicken from the oil and place them on soaked tissue papers to drain excess oil.

IV. Sauté the onions: In the same wok, add some more oil and sauté the onions until they turn translucent and lightly browned.

V. Add the green chilies: Introduce the green chilies to the wok and cook for about a minute, allowing their flavors to infuse into the dish.

VI. Season the dish: Add salt, soy sauce, and vinegar to the wok, mixing them well with the onions and chilies.

VII. Combine the chicken: Add the deep-fried chicken pieces to the wok and toss everything together, ensuring the chicken is evenly coated with the flavorsome sauce.

VIII. Serve and enjoy: Transfer the Chilli Chicken to a serving dish. Garnish with fresh cilantro or spring onions if desired. Serve hot and savor the delicious flavors!

Cooking notes:

I. Adjust the amount of green chilies according to your desired level of spiciness.

II. For a healthier alternative, you can also opt to pan-fry or bake the chicken instead of deep frying.

III. Feel free to add additional vegetables such as bell peppers, onions, or spring onions to the dish for added texture and flavor.

IV. Serve the Chilli Chicken as an appetizer, alongside steamed rice, or as part of a stir-fry noodle dish.

V. Enjoy the tantalizing flavors of your homemade Chilli Chicken!

4. Vietnamese Dumplings

Vietnamese dumplings are made with rice flour, salt, and water, and it has a filling of shrimp, pork, mung beans, onions, salt & pepper. Traditionally, they are wrapped in banana leaves and steamed with oil. These dumplings are usually served with fish sauce and eaten with onions.

Serve: 20

Prep Time: 40 Minutes

List of Ingredients:

- 2 tablespoons of dried black fungus, chopped
- 2 small shallots, chopped
- 2 garlic cloves, minced
- 1 green chili, minced
- 1 teaspoon of pepper
- 1 tablespoon of corn flour
- 20-24 wonton wrappers
- 18 oz of pork, minced
- 2 cloves, minced
- Coriander leaves, a handful
- 1 teaspoon of salt
- 2 tablespoons of oil
- 2 tablespoons of water

For garnishing

- 1/25 cucumber, sliced
- 5 shallots, chopped

Method:

I. Prepare the filling: In a bowl, combine pork, chili, shallots, fungus, garlic, coriander leaves, salt, and pepper. Mix well to incorporate all the ingredients.

II. Stir-fry the filling: Heat oil in a pan and stir-fry the pork mixture for approximately 5 minutes, until the pork is cooked through and the flavors are well combined.

III. Prepare the corn flour slurry: In a small bowl, mix corn flour and water to create a smooth slurry.

IV. Assemble the dumplings: Take a wonton wrapper and brush the edges with the corn flour slurry. Place a spoonful of the pork mixture in the center of the wrapper. Fold the wrapper to enclose the filling, shaping it into a sausage-like shape.

V. Steam the dumplings: Arrange the prepared dumplings in a steamer and steam them for about 6 minutes, or until the wrappers become translucent and the filling is fully cooked.

VI. Garnish and serve: Garnish the steamed dumplings with fried shallots and cucumber slices for added flavor and freshness. Serve them hot with a dipping sauce of your choice.

VII. Enjoy the Vietnamese Dumplings: Dive into the delightful flavors of the freshly steamed dumplings, savoring the combination of tender pork and aromatic ingredients.

Cooking notes:

I. You can customize the filling by adding additional ingredients like carrots, mushrooms, or water chestnuts for added texture and flavor.

II. If you prefer a spicier kick, feel free to adjust the amount of chili or add other spicy ingredients like sriracha or chili sauce to the filling.

III. Vietnamese dumplings are often enjoyed with a tangy dipping sauce made with a combination of soy sauce, lime juice, garlic, and chili. You can also serve them with a variety of Asian sauces such as hoisin sauce or fish sauce.

IV. Steaming the dumplings helps retain their moisture and results in a tender and juicy texture. Ensure the steamer is properly set up and the water is boiling before placing the dumplings in it.

V. Enjoy the delightful flavors and textures of your homemade Vietnamese Dumplings!

5. Hazelnut Asian Lettuce Wrap

Hazelnut Asian lettuce wrap is a unique, delicious, and very healthy Asian recipe. It has a zesty sauce with chicken and mixed with hazelnut, and coleslaw and wrapped with romaine leaves.

Serve: 2

Prep Time: 45 Minutes

List of Ingredients:

- 2 teaspoons of garlic, minced
- 1/3 cup of orange juice
- 1/2 tablespoon of soy sauce
- 1 tablespoon of rice wine
- 1 cup of hazelnut, toasted
- 1/2 cup of green onions, sliced
- 2 romaine leaves
- 1 tablespoon of oil
- 26 oz of chicken, minced
- 1/3 cup of hoisin sauce
- 1 tablespoon of ginger, minced
- 4 cups of coleslaw mix
- 1/4 cup of cilantro leaves

vvvvvvvvvvvvvvvvvvvvvvvvvvvv

Method:

I. Heat oil in a pan: Begin by heating oil in a pan over medium heat.

II. Sauté chicken and garlic: Add the chicken and garlic to the pan and sauté them together for approximately 10 minutes, or until the chicken is cooked through and the garlic becomes fragrant.

III. Prepare the sauce: To the pan, add orange juice, ginger, soy sauce, hoisin sauce, vinegar, and 1/3 cup of hazelnuts. Stir everything together and let the flavors meld.

IV. Blend the sauce: Transfer the mixture from the pan into a blender. Blend until you achieve a smooth puree consistency.

V.   Coat the chicken with the sauce: Pour the sauce over the cooked chicken in the pan, ensuring it is fully coated.

VI.   Add the remaining ingredients: To the pan, add green onions, coleslaw, cilantro, and the remaining hazelnuts.

VII.   Mix everything well: Toss and mix all the ingredients in the pan until they are well combined and evenly coated with the sauce.

VIII.   Serve and enjoy: Spoon the flavorful mixture into lettuce leaves, wrap them up, and savor the delicious Hazelnut Asian Wrap.

Cooking notes:

I.   Adjust the seasoning: Taste the sauce and adjust the amount of soy sauce, hoisin sauce, or vinegar according to your preference.

II.   Texture variations: Feel free to add other vegetables or toppings like carrots, bell peppers, or crispy noodles for added crunch and texture.

III.   Lettuce options: You can use different types of lettuce, such as butter lettuce or romaine hearts, as a wrap for the filling.

IV.   Serving suggestions: Serve the Hazelnut Asian Wrap as a light and refreshing appetizer or as a main dish alongside rice or noodles.

V.   Enjoy the delightful combination of flavors in your homemade Hazelnut Asian Wrap!

6. Crab Rangoon Dip

Crab Rangoon dip creamiest and cheesy dip to enjoy crispy chips. It's simple to make, cheesy and has rich flavors of cream cheese and mayonnaise. It has crab meat, you can mix it with spices to enjoy a light dinner.

Serve: 8

Prep Time: 40 minutes

List of Ingredients:

- 1/4 cup of mayonnaise
- 1/4 cup of sour cream
- 12 oz of wonton wrappers
- 8 oz of cream cheese
- 12 oz of lump crab meat
- 1 cup of cheddar cheese, shredded
- 3 green onions, sliced
- 1 teaspoon of Worcestershire sauce
- 1 teaspoon of sesame oil
- 1/2 teaspoon of Sriracha,
- Salt and black pepper, to taste
- 1/4 cup of Parmesan cheese, grated
- 1 teaspoon of soy sauce
- 1/2 teaspoon of garlic powder

vvvvvvvvvvvvvvvvvvvvvvvvvvv

Method:

I. Preheat the oven: Preheat the oven to 350°F (175°C).

II. Prepare the wonton wrappers: Lightly coat the wonton wrappers with cooking spray.

III. Bake the wonton wrappers: Place the coated wonton wrappers in the preheated oven and bake for approximately 5 minutes, or until they turn golden and crispy. Keep an eye on them to prevent burning.

IV. Adjust the oven temperature: Increase the oven temperature to 450°F (230°C) for the next step.

V. Prepare the dip mixture: In a bowl, combine mayonnaise, cream cheese, and sour cream. Add crab meat, cheddar cheese, Parmesan cheese, green onions, sriracha sauce, soy sauce, Worcestershire sauce, sesame oil, garlic powder, and a pinch of salt and pepper. Mix everything well until fully combined.

VI. Spread the crab mixture: Transfer the prepared crab mixture into a baking dish, spreading it evenly to cover the bottom.

VII. Add a cheesy topping: Sprinkle some additional cheddar cheese on top of the crab mixture, adding an extra layer of deliciousness.

VIII. Bake the dip: Place the baking dish in the preheated oven and bake for approximately 25 minutes, or until the top is golden and bubbly, and the dip is heated through.

IX. Remove from the oven: Once cooked, carefully remove the baking dish from the oven using oven mitts or heat-resistant gloves.

X. Serve and enjoy: Serve the Crab Rangoon Dip warm and with your choice of dippers, such as wonton chips, crackers, or sliced vegetables.

Cooking notes:

I. Crab meat options: You can use fresh or canned crab meat for this recipe. Ensure that the crab meat is properly cooked and any shells or cartilage are removed.

II. Customizing the spice level: Adjust the amount of sriracha sauce according to your preferred level of spiciness.

III. Dipping sauce variations: You can serve the dip with additional sauces such as sweet chili sauce, plum sauce, or soy sauce for added flavor.

IV. Garnish ideas: Consider garnishing the dip with chopped green onions, sesame seeds, or a drizzle of sriracha for added visual appeal.

V. Enjoy the irresistible flavors of your homemade Crab Rangoon Dip!

7. Japanese Prawn Tempura

Japanese prawn tempura is a deep-fried prawn dish that is served with tempura sauce. This one is a crunchy appetizer to eat with your dinner. It has prawns, tempura flour, soybean oil, soy sauce, and mirin.

Serve: 4

Prep Time: 40 minutes

List of Ingredients:

- 20 prawns
- 180 ml of ice cold water
- Salt, to taste
- Tempura sauce, as needed
- ½ cup of soya sauce
- 5 cups of Mirin
- 1 cup of water
- 14 oz of Japanese tempura flour
- Soybean oil, for frying
- 5 cups of sake

vvvvvvvvvvvvvvvvvvvvvvvvvvvvvv

Method:

I. Prepare the batter: In a medium bowl, mix water with tempura sauce and salt to create a batter. Stir until the ingredients are well combined.

II. Chill the batter: Place the batter in the refrigerator for about 15-30 minutes. Chilling the batter helps achieve a crispy texture when frying.

III. Heat oil for frying: Heat a sufficient amount of oil in a deep pan or fryer until it reaches a temperature of around 350°F (180°C).

IV. Coat the shrimp: Dip each shrimp into the chilled tempura batter, ensuring it is fully coated.

V. Deep fry the shrimp: Carefully place the battered shrimp into the hot oil and fry them until they turn golden brown and crispy. Fry them in small batches to ensure even cooking.

VI. Drain excess oil: Once cooked, remove the shrimp from the oil using a slotted spoon or tongs, allowing any excess oil to drain off. Place them on a paper towel-lined plate to absorb any remaining oil.

VII. Serve with tempura sauce: Arrange the cooked prawn tempura on a serving platter and serve it with a side of tempura sauce for dipping.

VIII. Garnish and optional sides: Consider garnishing the prawn tempura with some sesame seeds or finely chopped green onions for added flavor and visual appeal. You can also serve it with a side of grated daikon radish or a sprinkle of shichimi togarashi (Japanese seven spice) for an extra kick.

IX. Accompaniments: Prawn tempura is often enjoyed with a side of steamed rice, a bowl of miso soup, and a variety of pickled vegetables for a complete Japanese meal experience.

X. Enjoy the Japanese Prawn Tempura: Delight in the light and crispy texture of the prawn tempura, savoring the flavors of the perfectly fried shrimp.

Cooking notes:

I. Ensure that the shrimp are cleaned, deveined, and patted dry before coating them in the tempura batter.

II. For optimal results, maintain the oil temperature throughout the frying process by adjusting the heat as needed.

III. To achieve a lighter and crispier tempura batter, you can use a combination of all-purpose flour and cornstarch in a 1:1 ratio.

IV. Experiment with other vegetables like sweet potatoes, zucchini, or bell peppers, which can also be coated and fried in the same tempura batter.

V. Enjoy the prawn tempura immediately after cooking to fully experience its crispiness. Over time, the texture may soften.

VI. Indulge in the delectable flavors and crispy texture of your homemade Japanese Prawn Tempura!

8. Pineapple Fried Rice

Enjoy an island vibe with this lovely delectable pineapple fried rice. This rice is made with lots of flavors, and vegetables and feels fancy to enjoy during your lunchtime.

Serve: 4

Prep Time: 20 minutes

List of Ingredients:

- 1 onion, chopped
- 1/4 cup of cashews, chopped
- 3 cups of cooked rice
- Juice of 1 lemon
- 2 tablespoons of soy sauce
- 1 teaspoon of Sriracha
- 2 green onions, sliced
- 2 tablespoons of coconut oil
- 1 red bell pepper, diced
- 1 cup of pineapple, diced
- 3 cloves of garlic, minced
- 1/2 cup of peas, frozen
- 2 eggs, beaten

vvvvvvvvvvvvvvvvvvvvvvvvvvvv

Method:

I. Heat oil in a skillet over medium heat. Add onions, bell peppers, and pineapple. Sauté until the vegetables are softened and the pineapple is slightly caramelized.

II. Add cashews and garlic to the skillet. Cook for about 1 minute, stirring continuously, until fragrant.

III. Add cooked rice and peas to the skillet. Drizzle with lemon juice, soy sauce, and Sriracha sauce. Stir well to combine all the ingredients.

IV. Push the rice mixture to one side of the skillet, creating a space for the eggs. Crack the eggs into the empty space and scramble them. Once the eggs are partially cooked, mix them into the rice.

V. Garnish the pineapple fried rice with chopped green onions for a fresh finish.

VI. Serve the pineapple fried rice hot as a delicious main dish or as a side to accompany your favorite Asian-inspired meals.

Cooking Notes:

I. Use cold, cooked rice: To prevent the rice from sticking together, it's best to use cold, cooked rice that has been refrigerated for a few hours or overnight. This helps to maintain a firmer texture when stir-frying.

II. Customize your fried rice: Feel free to add additional ingredients such as cooked shrimp, chicken, or tofu to enhance the protein content. You can also include other vegetables like carrots, peas, or corn for added color and nutritional variety.

III. Adjust seasonings to taste: The amounts of lemon juice, soy sauce, and Sriracha sauce can be adjusted according to your preference. Start with smaller amounts and gradually add more to achieve the desired level of tanginess, saltiness, and spiciness.

IV. Be cautious with the heat: If you prefer a milder flavor, reduce the amount of Sriracha sauce or omit it altogether. If you enjoy spicy flavors, increase the amount or add additional chili flakes for an extra kick.

V. Handle the rice with care: When stirring the rice, use a gentle tossing motion to prevent it from becoming mushy. This helps to maintain the individual grains and ensures a pleasant texture.

VI. Serve immediately: Pineapple fried rice is best served fresh and hot. It's recommended to serve it immediately after cooking to fully enjoy its flavors and textures. Leftovers can be refrigerated for up to 2 days but note that the rice may lose some of its crispness.

VII. Enjoy the vibrant flavors and textures of this delightful Pineapple Fried Rice as a satisfying meal or a delightful side dish in your Asian-inspired culinary adventures!

9. Grilled Fish South-East Asian Dressing

Grilled fish with a South-East Asian dressing will melt in your mouth and serve with Asian dressing. This platter tastes sweet and tangy and garnished with red chilies and coriander.

Serve: 4

Prep Time: 40 Minutes

List of Ingredients:

- 10 ml of fish sauce
- 1 tablespoon of sugar
- 7 oz of fish filet
- 10 ml of sesame oil
- 30 ml of rice vinegar
- Salt, to taste
- A handful of raw garlic
- 1 oz of coriander leaf, chopped
- 7 oz of sugar
- A handful of red chili, chopped

vvvvvvvvvvvvvvvvvvvvvvvvvvvvvv

Method:

I. Prepare the marinade: In a bowl, combine sesame oil, fish sauce, and sugar. Mix well to dissolve the sugar and create a flavorful marinade.

II. Marinate the fish: Place the fish in the marinade, ensuring it is coated on all sides. Allow it to marinate in the refrigerator for 20 minutes, allowing the flavors to penetrate the fish.

III. Preheat the grill: Heat the grill to medium-high heat.

IV. Grill the fish: Place the marinated fish on the preheated grill and cook it for a few minutes on each side until it is cooked through and has grill marks. The exact cooking time will depend on the thickness of the fish filets or whole fish.

V. Prepare the South-East Asian dressing: In a small pot, combine sugar, rice vinegar, salt, and raw garlic. Bring the mixture to a boil and simmer for 1-2 minutes, allowing the flavors to meld together.

VI. Remove the fish from the grill: Carefully remove the grilled fish from the grill and transfer it to a serving plate or platter.

VII. Drizzle with the South-East Asian dressing: Pour the prepared South-East Asian dressing over the grilled fish, ensuring it coats the fish evenly.

VIII. Garnish and serve: Garnish the dish with fresh herbs such as cilantro or Thai basil, and sliced chili peppers for added flavor and presentation. Serve the grilled fish with steamed rice or a side of Asian-inspired vegetables.

IX. Enjoy the Grilled Fish with South-East Asian Dressing: Savor the succulent fish with its aromatic marinade and flavorful dressing.

Cooking notes:

I. Fish selection: Choose firm-fleshed fish varieties like salmon, snapper, or sea bass for grilling as they hold up well on the grill.

II. Adjusting the marinade: Feel free to adjust the marinade ingredients to suit your taste preferences. Add a squeeze of lime juice or a splash of soy sauce for an extra tangy or savory note.

III. Grilling tips: Ensure the grill is well-oiled or use a grilling basket or foil to prevent the fish from sticking. Monitor the cooking time carefully to avoid overcooking the fish.

IV. Enhancing the dressing: Experiment with additional ingredients like lime zest, ginger, or chili sauce to customize the South-East Asian dressing to your liking.

V. Enjoy the delectable combination of grilled fish and the vibrant flavors of the South-East Asian dressing in this delightful and flavorful dish!

10. Stir Fry Udon Noodles with Black Pepper Sauce

This dish is a thick noodle used in Japanese cuisine. The flavorsome preparation is quite easy with black pepper, bell peppers, mock duck, and black pepper sauce. This is a perfect appetizer to enjoy in the evening.

Serve: 2

Prep Time: 45 Minutes

List of Ingredients:

- ½ piece of green capsicum
- ½ piece of red capsicum
- A handful of spring onion
- 1 tablespoon of black pepper
- 7 oz of udon noodles
- 1 red onion
- ½ piece of yellow capsicum
- 2 oz of bean sprouts
- 5 oz of mock duck

For sauce

- 2 tablespoons of minced ginger
- 25 ml of soy sauce
- 20 ml of peanut oil
- 25 ml of sesame oil
- 2 minced garlic cloves
- 30 ml of rice vinegar

vvvvvvvvvvvvvvvvvvvvvvvvvvvvvvvvv

Method:

I. Prepare the sauce: In a small bowl, combine all the ingredients for the sauce. Mix well until the flavors are fully incorporated.

II. Heat oil in a pan or wok over medium heat.

III. Add the udon noodles to the pan and sprinkle with black pepper. Stir-fry for a few minutes until the noodles are heated through and evenly coated with the black pepper.

IV. Add the green, yellow, and red capsicum (bell peppers) along with the mock duck or any other desired protein. Stir-fry for a few more minutes until the capsicum is slightly softened.

V. Pour the prepared sauce over the noodles and vegetables in the pan. Toss everything together to ensure the sauce is evenly distributed and coats the ingredients.

VI. Add the bean sprouts to the pan and continue to stir-fry for another minute or two until the bean sprouts are slightly wilted.

VII. Increase the heat to high and continue tossing the noodles and vegetables for another minute or two, allowing the flavors to meld and the dish to become well combined.

VIII. Remove the pan from the heat and transfer the stir-fried udon noodles to serving bowls.

IX. Garnish the noodles with additional toppings such as chopped spring onions or cilantro for added freshness and visual appeal.

X. Serve the stir-fry udon noodles with black pepper sauce hot and enjoy this delicious and flavorful dish!

Cooking Notes:

I. Noodle Variations: Feel free to use your preferred type of udon noodles - fresh, dried, or frozen - according to availability and personal preference. Follow the package instructions for cooking times and adjust accordingly.

II. Adjusting Spice Level: If you prefer a spicier dish, you can add a pinch of chili flakes or a drizzle of chili oil to the black pepper sauce.

III. Protein Options: Aside from mock duck, you can use other protein sources such as tofu, seitan, or sliced chicken or beef to add more texture and flavor to the dish.

IV. Vegetable Variations: Customize the stir-fry by adding or substituting other vegetables like carrots, broccoli, or snap peas. Just ensure that the vegetables are thinly sliced or cut into bite-sized pieces for even cooking.

V. Sauce Balance: Taste the sauce before adding it to the noodles and adjust the flavors as needed. You can add a bit more soy sauce for saltiness, honey or sugar for sweetness, or rice vinegar for acidity.

VI. Quick and High-Heat Cooking: Stir-fries are best cooked quickly over high heat to preserve the freshness and texture of the ingredients. Have all the ingredients prepared and ready to go before starting the cooking process.

VII. Enjoy the enticing flavors and delightful textures of this Stir Fry Udon Noodles with Black Pepper Sauce dish as a satisfying and satisfying meal!

11. Thai Fish Curry

Thai fish curry is a delectable fish dish that is easy to make and can be made in 40 minutes. It is packed with rich flavors like Thai green curry paste, garlic, ginger, and coconut milk. The lemon and basil leaves add a super refreshing taste to the Thai curry.

Serve: 2

Prep Time: 50 minutes

List of Ingredients:

- 1 tablespoon of Thai green curry paste
- 1 teaspoon of garlic, chopped
- 1 teaspoon of ginger, chopped
- 2 tablespoons of coriander, chopped
- 2 tablespoons of lemon juice
- 3-4 basil leaves
- To taste salt & pepper
- 35 oz of fish, cubed
- 1 tablespoon of oil
- 2 tablespoons of onions, chopped
- 1 teaspoon of coconut milk
- 1 tablespoon of palm sugar

vvvvvvvvvvvvvvvvvvvvvvvvvvvvvv

Method:

I. Marinate the fish cubes: In a bowl, coat the fish cubes with Thai green curry paste, lime juice, salt, and pepper. Allow them to marinate for some time to infuse the flavors.

II. Heat oil in a pan: Place a pan over medium heat and add oil. Allow it to heat up.

III. Sauté the aromatics: Add the onions, ginger, and garlic to the pan. Sauté them for 2-3 minutes until they become fragrant and slightly softened.

IV. Cook the curry paste: Stir in the remaining Thai green curry paste and cook for 2 minutes to release its flavor.

V. Add coconut milk and fish cubes: Pour in the coconut milk and add some of the marinated fish cubes to the pan. Cook for 2 minutes to allow the fish to cook through and absorb the flavors of the curry.

VI. Season and garnish: Add the chopped coriander, lime juice, and palm sugar to the curry. Stir well to incorporate the ingredients. Taste and adjust the seasoning if needed.

VII. Garnish with basil leaves: Sprinkle some fresh basil leaves over the curry to add a fragrant and herbaceous note.

VIII. Serve with rice: Transfer the Thai fish curry to a serving dish and serve it alongside steamed rice or your preferred choice of grains.

IX. Enjoy the Thai Fish Curry: Dive into the delicious blend of flavors, from the creamy coconut milk to the aromatic spices and tender fish.

Cooking notes:

I. Fish selection: Choose firm-fleshed fish varieties like cod, tilapia, or snapper for the curry, as they hold up well during the cooking process.

II. Thai green curry paste: You can use store-bought Thai green curry paste or make your own from scratch using a combination of ingredients like green chilies, lemongrass, garlic, shallots, and spices. Adjust the amount of curry paste according to your preferred level of spiciness.

III. Adjusting the spice level: If you prefer a milder curry, reduce the amount of Thai green curry paste or omit the fresh chilies. On the other hand, if you like it spicier, add extra curry paste or sliced Thai bird's eye chilies.

IV. Coconut milk: Choose full-fat coconut milk for a creamier and richer curry. If desired, you can also use a combination of coconut milk and coconut cream for added richness.

V. Additional vegetables: Feel free to add vegetables like bell peppers, eggplant, or bamboo shoots to the curry for added texture and flavor. Just adjust the cooking time accordingly to ensure they are cooked through.

VI. Indulge in the tantalizing flavors of this Thai Fish Curry, which combines aromatic spices, creamy coconut milk, and succulent fish for a truly satisfying meal.

12. Sweet & Sour Chicken

Sweet and sour chicken with crispy chicken and bell peppers tastes like heaven. It has all the spices like pepper, garlic, and honey for a sweet taste. The chicken breast cubes are first coated and then fried. Looks super awesome!

Serve: 4

Prep Time: 10 minutes

List of Ingredients:

- 1/2 cup of cornstarch
- Salt, to taste
- 2 tablespoons of oil
- 1/3 cup of honey
- 2 tablespoons of soy sauce
- 1/4 cup of ketchup
- 2 cloves of garlic, minced
- 16 oz of chicken breast, cut into 1/2" cubes
- Ground black pepper, to taste
- 2 eggs, beaten
- 2 bell peppers, sliced
- 1/2 cup of apple cider vinegar

vvvvvvvvvvvvvvvvvvvvvvvvvvvvvvv

Method:

I. Prepare the chicken: In a bowl, season the chicken with salt.

II. Coat the chicken: Add cornstarch to the bowl and coat the chicken thoroughly with it, ensuring each piece is evenly coated.

III. Mix with eggs: In the same bowl, mix the chicken with beaten eggs, allowing the mixture to adhere to the chicken pieces.

IV. Heat oil in a skillet: Place a skillet or wok over medium-high heat and heat oil.

V. Cook the chicken: Add the coated chicken to the skillet and cook for about 5 minutes, turning the pieces to ensure they are cooked on all sides and have a crispy exterior.

VI. Sauté bell peppers: Add the bell peppers to the skillet and sauté them until they become soft and slightly tender.

VII. Prepare the sauce: In a separate bowl, mix together apple cider vinegar, soy sauce, honey, ketchup, and minced garlic to create the sweet and sour sauce.

VIII. Add the sauce: Pour the prepared sauce into the skillet with the chicken and bell peppers.

IX. Simmer and cook: Allow the chicken, bell peppers, and sauce to simmer together for about 5 minutes, ensuring the flavors blend and the chicken is cooked through.

X. Serve warm: Transfer the sweet and sour chicken to a serving dish and serve it warm alongside rice or your preferred choice of grains.

XI. Enjoy the Sweet and Sour Chicken: Indulge in the delicious combination of crispy chicken, tangy sweet and sour sauce, and the vibrant flavors of bell peppers.

Cooking Notes:

I.   Chicken selection: Use boneless, skinless chicken breasts or chicken thighs for this recipe, as they are more tender and cook quickly.

II. Cornstarch coating: Coating the chicken with cornstarch helps create a crispy texture. It also helps seal in the juices, keeping the chicken moist.

III. Adjusting the sauce: Taste the sauce and adjust the sweetness or tanginess according to your preference by adding more honey or vinegar.

IV. Vegetable variations: Feel free to add other vegetables like onions, pineapple chunks, or carrots to the dish for added texture and flavor.

V.   Garnish options: For an extra burst of freshness, you can garnish the dish with chopped scallions or sesame seeds.

VI. Savor the delightful combination of sweet and tangy flavors in this homemade Sweet and Sour Chicken. The crispy chicken, colorful bell peppers, and irresistible sauce create a dish that will satisfy your cravings. Enjoy it as a main course with rice or noodles for a complete meal.

13. Stir-Fried Brussels Sprouts

Stir-fried Brussels sprouts are an awesome dish with garlic and pepper. This recipe gets ready in just 10 minutes and is the best breakfast dish. Sprouts are nutritious and packed with protein. It is seasoned with the perfect balance of spices and sauces.

Serve: 3

Prep Time: 20 minutes

List of Ingredients:

- ¾ teaspoon of salt

- 1 teaspoon of soy sauce

- 2 cups of Brussels Sprouts

- ½ cup of red pepper

- 4-5 cloves of garlic

- 2 tablespoons of sesame oil

- Cilantro, for garnishing

- 2 teaspoons of Lee Kum Kee vegetarian stir fry sauce

- 1 1/4 teaspoons of rock salt

- Green onions, for garnishing

- Chili oil: 1 teaspoon

vvvvvvvvvvvvvvvvvvvvvvvvvvvvv

Method:

I. Heat oil in a pan: Place a pan or wok over medium-high heat and heat the oil.

II. Add Brussels sprouts: Add the Brussels sprouts to the pan and cook for a few minutes, stirring occasionally, until they start to brown and become slightly tender.

III. Add chili oil and garlic: Drizzle chili oil over the Brussels sprouts and add minced garlic to the pan. Continue to sauté for a minute or two until the garlic becomes fragrant.

IV. Season with pepper: Sprinkle some freshly ground black pepper over the sprouts, adjusting the amount according to your taste preferences.

V. Add salt and stir fry sauce: Sprinkle salt over the sprouts and then add Lee Kum Kee vegetarian stir fry sauce and soy sauce. Toss the sprouts to coat them evenly with the sauce.

VI. Let the sprouts absorb the sauce: Allow the Brussels sprouts to cook for a few more minutes, stirring occasionally, until they have absorbed the flavors of the sauce and become tender yet still slightly crisp.

VII. Turn off the flame: Once the Brussels sprouts are cooked to your desired level of tenderness, turn off the heat.

VIII. Garnish with green onions and cilantro: Sprinkle chopped green onions and fresh cilantro over the stir-fried Brussels sprouts to add a burst of freshness and aroma.

IX. Stir-fried Brussels sprouts are ready: Transfer the stir-fried Brussels sprouts to a serving dish.

X. Serve hot: Serve the dish immediately while it's still hot, as Brussels sprouts tend to taste best when served fresh and warm.

XI. Enjoy your Stir-Fried Brussels Sprouts: Enjoy the delicious and flavorful combination of tender Brussels sprouts with a hint of heat from the chili oil and a savory note from the stir fry sauce.

Cooking Notes:

I. Brussels sprouts selection: Choose fresh Brussels sprouts that are firm, without any discoloration or soft spots.

II. Slicing the sprouts: For faster and more even cooking, consider slicing the Brussels sprouts in half or into thin slices.

III. Adjusting the heat: If you prefer a spicier flavor, you can add more chili oil or red pepper flakes to the dish.

IV. Customizing the sauce: Feel free to adjust the amount of stir fry sauce and soy sauce according to your taste preferences. You can also add other seasonings or spices to enhance the flavor.

V. Texture preferences: Cook the Brussels sprouts to your desired level of tenderness. Some may prefer them more crisp, while others may prefer them softer.

VI. Serving suggestions: Stir-fried Brussels sprouts make a great side dish for various meals. They can be served alongside grilled chicken, roasted salmon, or as a component in stir-fry noodles or fried rice.

VII. Enjoy the delicious and nutritious Stir-Fried Brussels Sprouts, packed with flavor and nutrients. This dish showcases the natural sweetness and slight bitterness of Brussels sprouts, complemented by the savory and spicy elements of the sauce. It's a versatile and satisfying dish that can be enjoyed as a side or a main course.

14. Chinese Silky Egg Pudding

Chinese silky egg pudding is a delicious, smooth, and unique dessert dish. It's a 3-ingredient dessert that has rich egg content and steamy perfection.

Serve: 3

Prep Time: 45 minutes

List of Ingredients:

- 2 cups of water
- 4 oz of rock sugar
- 5 whole eggs

Method:

I. Whisk eggs: In a bowl, whisk the eggs until they are well beaten.

II. Melt rock sugar: In a separate pot, bring water to a boil and melt the rock sugar in the hot boiling water. Stir until the sugar is completely dissolved.

III. Combine sugar and eggs: Pour the dissolved sugar into the bowl with the beaten eggs. Mix well to combine the sugar and eggs.

IV. Strain the mixture: Pour the mixture into a jug or container through a sieve to remove any lumps or impurities.

V. Prepare the steamer: Set up your steamer by filling it with water and bringing it to a simmer.

VI. Steam the pudding: Place the bowls or ramekins containing the egg mixture into the steamer. Cover the steamer and steam the pudding for approximately 10 minutes.

VII. Slow cooking process: After steaming for 10 minutes, turn off the steamer but leave the bowls inside. Allow the pudding to continue cooking slowly in the residual heat for an additional 30 minutes. This slow cooking process helps create a smooth and silky texture.

VIII. Remove from steamer: Carefully remove the bowls from the steamer using oven mitts or a towel, as they will be hot.

IX. Let it cool: Allow the pudding to cool at room temperature for a while before transferring it to the refrigerator.

X. Chill in the refrigerator: Place the bowls of pudding in the refrigerator and let them chill for at least a couple of hours, or until fully set and chilled.

XI. Chinese silky egg pudding is ready: Once the pudding is fully set, it is ready to be enjoyed.

Cooking Notes:

I. Type of sugar: Traditional Chinese silky egg pudding is made with rock sugar, but you can use regular granulated sugar as a substitute.

II. Texture: The key to achieving a silky smooth texture is to whisk the eggs thoroughly and strain the mixture to remove any lumps.

III. Steaming time: Steaming time may vary depending on the size and depth of the bowls or ramekins you use. Adjust the steaming time accordingly to ensure the pudding is fully cooked and set.

IV. Cooling and chilling: Allowing the pudding to cool at room temperature before refrigeration helps prevent condensation from forming on the surface of the pudding.

V. Serving suggestions: Chinese silky egg pudding can be served chilled as a refreshing dessert on its own, or you can top it with a drizzle of caramel sauce, fresh fruits, or a sprinkle of crushed nuts for added flavor and texture.

VI. Enjoy the luscious and silky-smooth texture of this traditional Chinese dessert. The combination of eggs and sugar creates a delicate and lightly sweetened pudding that melts in your mouth. Whether enjoyed on its own or with additional toppings, Chinese silky egg pudding is a delightful treat for any occasion.

15. Beef Jerky

Beef Jerky is a chewy and flavorful protein snack. It is made with lots of flavors – spicy and sweet. This dish is mixed with soy sauce, five-spice powder, sugar, rice wine, and chili powder. A power-packed delicious snack recipe for midday hunger.

Serve: 2-4

Prep Time: 25 minutes

List of Ingredients:

- 4 tablespoons of soy sauce
- 3 tablespoons of sugar
- 1 tablespoon of rice wine
- 1/2 cup of water
- 1 tablespoon of sesame seeds
- 1 tablespoon of chili powder
- 17 oz of lean beef, thick strips
- 1 teaspoon of five-spice powder
- 3 tablespoons of oil
- Salt, to taste

Method:

I. Prepare the marinade: In a bowl, mix together soy sauce, sugar, rice wine, five spice powder, and water. Stir until the sugar is dissolved.

II. Marinate the beef: Add the beef strips to the marinade, ensuring they are well coated. Cover the bowl and refrigerate overnight to allow the flavors to infuse into the meat.

III. Preheat the oven: Preheat the oven to 320°F (160°C).

IV. Arrange the beef strips: Place the marinated beef strips on a baking tray, making sure they are evenly spaced out.

V. Bake in the oven: Bake the beef strips in the preheated oven for approximately 20 minutes. This will help dry out the meat and give it a chewy texture.

VI. Cook in a saucepan: Heat oil in a saucepan over medium heat. Add the marinated beef strips, along with any remaining marinade. Season with salt to taste and add chili powder for additional flavor, if desired.

VII. Sauté the beef: Cook the beef strips in the saucepan for about 5 minutes, stirring occasionally, until they are cooked through and slightly caramelized.

VIII. Turn off the heat: Once the beef strips are cooked to your desired level of doneness, turn off the flame.

IX. Let it cool: Allow the beef jerky to cool down before serving or storing.

X. Slice or serve as is: You can either slice the beef jerky into thin strips for snacking or serve it as whole pieces.

XI. Beef jerky is ready: Your homemade beef jerky is now ready to enjoy!

Cooking Notes:

I.   Beef selection: Choose lean cuts of beef, such as flank steak or sirloin, for making beef jerky.

II. Marinating time: Marinating the beef overnight allows the flavors to penetrate the meat and enhances the taste of the jerky.

III. Oven temperature: Adjust the oven temperature and cooking time as needed based on the thickness of your beef strips. Thinner strips may require less cooking time, while thicker strips may need more time to fully dry out.

IV. Storage: Once cooled, store the beef jerky in an airtight container or resealable bag. It can be kept at room temperature for a few days or refrigerated for longer shelf life.

V.   Flavor variations: Feel free to experiment with different spices and seasonings to customize the flavor of your beef jerky. Popular options include garlic powder, onion powder, black pepper, or even adding a touch of liquid smoke for a smoky flavor.

VI. Enjoy the savory and chewy goodness of homemade beef jerky as a protein-packed snack or a tasty addition to your favorite recipes. Whether you're on-the-go or simply looking for a flavorful treat, beef jerky is a versatile and satisfying option.

16. Teriyaki Salmon and Broccoli Bowls

Teriyaki salmon and broccoli is the craziest, most tasty, and complete meal with easy teriyaki sauce, steamed broccoli and rice. It's spicy, tangy, and sweet mixed with salmon, broccoli, and teriyaki sauce. This is a perfect Asian recipe to enjoy with family.

Serve: 4

Prep Time: 40 minutes

List of Ingredients:

- 3 cloves of garlic, minced
- 1 tablespoon of cornstarch
- 1/4 cup of soy sauce
- 1 tablespoon of freshly grated ginger
- 5 oz of salmon filets
- 2 oz of broccoli florets
- 1 cup of white rice
- 1/4 cup of brown sugar
- 2 tablespoons of honey

vvvvvvvvvvvvvvvvvvvvvvvvvvvvvv

Method:

I. Cook the rice: In a pan, add 1.5 cups of water and cook the rice according to the package instructions. Once cooked, set it aside.

II. Prepare the cornstarch mixture: In a small bowl, combine cornstarch and water, stirring until the cornstarch is dissolved. Set it aside.

III. Make the teriyaki sauce: In a saucepan, combine soy sauce, brown sugar, garlic, ginger, honey, and water. Bring the mixture to a simmer over medium heat, stirring occasionally.

IV. Thicken the sauce: Add the cornstarch mixture to the saucepan and cook for 2 minutes, stirring constantly. The sauce will thicken and become glossy.

V. Preheat the oven: Preheat the oven to 400°F (200°C).

VI. Bake the salmon: Place the salmon filets in a baking dish and pour the prepared teriyaki sauce over them. Bake the salmon in the preheated oven for approximately 15 minutes, or until it flakes easily with a fork.

VII. Steam the broccoli: Place the broccoli florets in a steamer and steam them for about 5 minutes, until they are tender-crisp.

VIII. Assemble the bowls: Divide the cooked rice among serving bowls. Top each bowl with a portion of the baked teriyaki salmon and steamed broccoli.

IX. Garnish (optional): Sprinkle sesame seeds or chopped green onions on top for added flavor and presentation.

X. Serve and enjoy: Serve the teriyaki salmon and broccoli bowls while still warm, and savor the delicious combination of flavors.

XI. Teriyaki salmon and broccoli bowls are ready to be enjoyed!

Cooking Notes:

I. Salmon selection: Choose fresh or frozen salmon filets of your choice. Skin-on or skinless filets both work well for this recipe.

II. Teriyaki sauce customization: Feel free to adjust the sweetness or saltiness of the teriyaki sauce according to your preference. You can add more honey for a sweeter flavor or reduce the amount of soy sauce for a milder taste.

III. Rice variations: Use your favorite type of rice for the bowls, such as white rice, brown rice, or even quinoa for a healthier option.

IV. Steaming broccoli: If you don't have a steamer, you can blanch the broccoli florets in boiling water for a few minutes until they are tender-crisp.

V. Additional toppings: Customize your bowls with additional toppings like sliced avocado, shredded carrots, or pickled ginger for extra flavor and texture.

VI. Enjoy these delicious and wholesome teriyaki salmon and broccoli bowls, which combine the goodness of tender salmon, crisp broccoli, and flavorful teriyaki sauce over a bed of rice. It's a satisfying and nutritious meal that can be easily prepared at home.

17. Spicy Vietnamese Chicken Sandwiches

Spicy Vietnamese chicken sandwiches are tangy, spicy, and served with salty pickled onions. These sandwiches are packed with grilled chicken and flavored with soy sauce and mayonnaise. Plan a lovely dinner with your loved one with these sandwiches.

Serve: 6

Prep Time: 1 hour 30 minutes

List of Ingredients:

- 2 tablespoons of soy sauce
- 2 carrots, sliced
- 1/2 cup of pickled cocktail onions
- Sriracha sauce, for spreading
- Cilantro sprigs
- 3/4 boneless chicken breast
- 1 tablespoon of mayonnaise,
- 1 shallot, sliced
- 10 oz of baguette
- 1 cucumber, sliced

VVVVVVVVVVVVVVVVVVVVVVVVVVVVV

Method:

I. Marinate the chicken: In a bowl, toss the chicken with soy sauce, mayonnaise, and shallot until well coated. Cover the bowl and refrigerate for at least 30 minutes to marinate the chicken.

II. Prepare the carrot and pickled onion mixture: In another bowl, mix the grated carrot with the pickled onions. Allow the mixture to sit for at least an hour to allow the flavors to meld together.

III. Preheat the grill pan: Heat a grill pan over medium heat.

IV. Grill the chicken: Place the marinated chicken on the hot grill pan and cook until the chicken is cooked through and has a nice char, approximately 4-5 minutes per side.

V. Prepare the baguette: Slice the baguette lengthwise and spread mayonnaise on both sides of the bread. Then, drizzle Sriracha sauce over the mayonnaise to add a spicy kick.

VI. Assemble the sandwich: Layer the grilled chicken on one side of the baguette. Top the chicken with the carrot and pickled onion mixture.

VII. Close the sandwich: Place the other half of the baguette on top of the filling to close the sandwich.

VIII. Optional: Press the sandwich: If desired, wrap the sandwich tightly in parchment paper or foil and press it down with a heavy object for about 10 minutes to allow the flavors to meld together and the bread to become slightly crispy.

IX. Slice the sandwich: Using a sharp knife, slice the sandwich into individual servings.

X. Serve and enjoy: Serve the Spicy Vietnamese Chicken Sandwiches immediately and savor the delicious combination of flavors.

XI. Spicy Vietnamese Chicken Sandwiches are ready to be enjoyed!

Cooking Notes:

I. Chicken selection: You can use boneless, skinless chicken breasts or thighs for this recipe. Ensure that the chicken is cooked thoroughly to an internal temperature of 165°F (74°C).

II. Marinating time: For the best flavor, marinate the chicken for at least 30 minutes. However, if you have more time, marinating the chicken for longer will enhance the flavor even more.

III. Pickled onions: You can use store-bought pickled onions or make your own by thinly slicing red onions and soaking them in a mixture of vinegar, sugar, and salt for about an hour.

IV. Bread options: Traditional Vietnamese sandwiches, or banh mi, are made with French baguettes. However, you can use any type of bread that you prefer, such as ciabatta or a crusty roll.

V. Customization: Feel free to customize your sandwich by adding fresh herbs like cilantro or mint, sliced cucumbers, or a squeeze of lime juice for an extra burst of flavor.

VI. Enjoy these Spicy Vietnamese Chicken Sandwiches packed with bold flavors and contrasting textures. The marinated grilled chicken, tangy pickled onions, and crisp carrot come together in a delightful sandwich that will transport you to the streets of Vietnam.

18. Black Sesame Soup

Black sesame soup is a thick, saucy, and unique Asian recipe. It has a nutty fragrance and tastes awesome with rice. A healthy and perfect soup to include in your dinner menu!

Serve: 4

Prep Time: 15 minutes

List of Ingredients:

- 1 ½ cups of water
- 2 tablespoons of rice flour
- ½ cup of black sesame seeds powder
- 2 tablespoons of rice flour
- 2 tablespoons of honey

vvvvvvvvvvvvvvvvvvvvvvvvvvvvvvvv

Method:

I. Prepare the ingredients: In a saucepan, combine water, rice flour, and black sesame powder.

II. Stir and cook: Stir the mixture occasionally as you cook it over medium heat.

III. Add honey: After 10 minutes of cooking, add honey to the saucepan. Stir well to incorporate the sweetness.

IV. Remove from heat: Once the soup has thickened and reached your desired consistency, remove the saucepan from the heat.

V. Serve warm: Ladle the black sesame soup into serving bowls while it is still warm.

VI. Optional: Garnish with additional black sesame seeds or a sprinkle of powdered sugar for added visual appeal.

VII. Enjoy as is: The black sesame soup can be enjoyed on its own as a comforting and nutritious dessert.

VIII. Optional: Add toppings: If desired, you can add toppings such as sliced almonds, coconut flakes, or a drizzle of condensed milk to enhance the flavor and texture of the soup.

IX. Allow to cool slightly: Let the soup cool for a few minutes before serving to prevent burning your tongue.

X.   Stir before serving: Before serving, give the soup a gentle stir to ensure that the ingredients are evenly distributed.

XI.   Black Sesame Soup is ready to be savored!

Cooking Notes:

I.   Black sesame powder: You can find black sesame powder in Asian grocery stores or online. Alternatively, you can grind black sesame seeds into a fine powder using a spice grinder or mortar and pestle.

II.   Adjust sweetness: The amount of honey can be adjusted to suit your taste preferences. Feel free to add more or less honey to achieve the desired level of sweetness.

III.   Texture: The consistency of the soup can be adjusted by adding more or less water and rice flour. If you prefer a thicker soup, increase the amount of rice flour. If you prefer a thinner consistency, add more water.

IV.   Variations: You can customize the flavor of the black sesame soup by adding a pinch of salt, a dash of vanilla extract, or a sprinkle of cinnamon for additional depth of flavor.

V.   Nutritional benefits: Black sesame seeds are rich in essential minerals, healthy fats, and antioxidants. They are also a good source of calcium and iron.

VI.   Serving suggestions: Black sesame soup is commonly enjoyed as a dessert or sweet treat in Asian cuisine. It can be served warm or chilled, depending on personal preference.

VII.   Indulge in the rich and nutty flavors of Black Sesame Soup, a classic Asian dessert that is both comforting and nutritious. Whether enjoyed as a standalone treat or paired with your favorite toppings, this simple and delicious soup is sure to satisfy your sweet tooth.

19. Pork Ginger Potstickers

Pork ginger potstickers are super easy to prepare and so hearty and healthy for dinner choice. These potstickers are awesome as an appetizer, snack, or a light dinner. You can also make this dish for a date night with your partner and explore the flavors of taste in your partner's mouth.

Serve: 40

Prep Time: 30 minutes

List of Ingredients:

- 16 oz of ground pork
- 1 carrot, shredded
- 2 tablespoons of ginger, grated
- 2 tablespoons of soy sauce
- 2 teaspoons of sesame oil
- 1/4 teaspoon of white pepper
- 40 wonton wrappers
- 2 tablespoons of soy sauce
- 1 cup of cabbage, shredded
- 3 oz of mushrooms, diced
- 2 cloves of garlic, pressed
- 1 green onion, sliced
- 1 teaspoon of rice vinegar
- 2 tablespoons of vegetable oil

Method:

I. Prepare the filling: In a bowl, combine the ground pork, finely chopped cabbage, green onion, grated carrot, minced garlic, diced mushrooms, soy sauce, grated ginger, rice vinegar, and white pepper. Mix well until all the ingredients are thoroughly combined.

II. Assemble the dumplings: Lay the dumpling wrappers on a clean surface. Take approximately 1 tablespoon of the pork mixture and place it in the center of each wrapper.

III. Seal the dumplings: Moisten the edges of the dumpling wrappers with water. Fold the wrapper in half to create a half-moon shape, pressing the edges together to seal the dumpling. Pleat the edges if desired for a decorative touch.

IV. Heat oil in a pan: In a non-stick skillet or frying pan, heat a small amount of oil over medium-high heat.

V. Cook the potstickers: Place the assembled potstickers in the hot pan, ensuring they are not touching each other. Cook until the bottoms become golden brown, approximately 2-3 minutes.

VI. Add water and steam: Add a small amount of water to the pan, enough to cover the bottom. Immediately cover the pan with a lid and reduce the heat to medium-low. Allow the potstickers to steam for 5-6 minutes or until the filling is cooked through.

VII. Crisp the bottoms (optional): After steaming, remove the lid and increase the heat to medium-high. Allow the potstickers to cook for an additional 1-2 minutes or until the bottoms become crispy.

VIII. Serve with dipping sauce: Transfer the potstickers to a serving platter and serve hot. Accompany them with your favorite dipping sauce, such as soy sauce mixed with a splash of rice vinegar or chili oil.

IX. Optional: Garnish and serve: If desired, garnish the potstickers with chopped green onions or sesame seeds before serving for added flavor and visual appeal.

X. Enjoy and share: Serve the pork ginger potstickers as an appetizer or part of a meal. Encourage everyone to dip the potstickers in the sauce and savor the delicious combination of flavors.

Cooking Notes:

I. Wrappers: Look for round dumpling wrappers in the refrigerated section of your grocery store or consider making your own from scratch.

II. Filling variations: Feel free to customize the filling by adding other ingredients such as water chestnuts, bamboo shoots, or cilantro for added texture and flavor.

III. Freezing: If you have leftover potstickers, you can freeze them by placing them in a single layer on a baking sheet, then transfer them to a freezer-safe container once they are frozen. To cook frozen potstickers, follow the same cooking instructions, but increase the steaming time by a few minutes.

IV. Dipping sauce: Experiment with different dipping sauce combinations to find your favorite. Some popular options include soy sauce with sesame oil, chili oil, or black vinegar.

V. Serving suggestions: Potstickers can be enjoyed as a standalone appetizer or served with steamed rice and vegetables for a complete meal.

VI. Share the joy: Potstickers are often served as part of a shared meal or as a social gathering dish, so invite family and friends to enjoy the delightful flavors together.

VII. Indulge in the irresistible flavors of Pork Ginger Potstickers, filled with a savory pork and vegetable mixture. These dumplings are a classic favorite in Asian cuisine, and with a few simple steps, you can create a delicious homemade version. Whether enjoyed as an appetizer, snack, or part of a larger meal, these potstickers are sure to satisfy your cravings.

20. Vegan Poke Bowl

The vegan poke bowl is a gluten-free bowl with healthy veggies and is easy to make. It has all the nutrients like avocado, sweet potato, and radish. It gets ready in less than 30 minutes. Very quick to make and is best for diet food.

Serve: 2-4

Prep Time: 30 minutes

List of Ingredients:

- 1 cucumber, sliced
- 1 avocado, sliced
- 3 spring onions, sliced
- 1 tablespoon of sesame seeds, topping
- 3 cups of cooked & 1 cup of uncooked white rice
- 1 sweet potato, peeled
- 1 carrot, sliced
- ¼ cup of radishes, sliced

For making sauce

- 1 tablespoon of maple syrup
- ¼ to ⅓ cup of tamari
- 1 tablespoon of rice vinegar
- 1 tablespoon of chili paste
- 2 teaspoons of toasted sesame oil
- 1 teaspoon of ginger, minced
- 2 cloves of garlic, minced

Method:

I. Steam the potatoes: Place the potatoes in a steamer and steam for 5-7 minutes or until they are tender. Remove from heat and set aside.

II. Prepare the sauce: In a separate bowl, combine tamari (or soy sauce), chili paste, rice vinegar, maple syrup, and sesame oil. Mix well until all the ingredients are thoroughly combined to create the flavorful sauce.

III. Toss the potatoes in the sauce: Transfer the steamed potatoes to a bowl and pour the sauce over them. Gently toss the potatoes to coat them evenly with the sauce.

IV. Prepare the rice: Divide cooked rice among serving bowls, creating a base for the poke bowl.

V. Add the sweet potatoes: Place the sauce-coated sweet potatoes on top of the rice in each bowl.

VI. Add avocado slices: Arrange avocado slices on one side of the bowl.

VII. Add vegetables: Add your choice of fresh vegetables, such as cucumber, carrot, radish, or edamame, to the other side of the bowl.

VIII. Drizzle with sauce: Drizzle additional sauce over the ingredients in each bowl, adjusting the amount to your preference.

IX. Top with sesame seeds and mayo: Sprinkle sesame seeds over the bowl for added texture and flavor. If desired, add a dollop of vegan mayo for extra creaminess.

X. Optional: Garnish and customize: Feel free to add additional toppings such as sliced scallions, pickled ginger, nori strips, or crushed peanuts for extra flavor and visual appeal.

XI. Enjoy your Vegan Poke Bowl: Serve the bowls immediately and enjoy the vibrant colors, textures, and flavors of this delicious and nutritious vegan poke bowl.

Cooking Notes:

I.   Rice selection: Use your favorite type of rice for the base, such as sushi rice, brown rice, or quinoa, to suit your dietary preferences.

II.   Sauce customization: Adjust the amount of chili paste and maple syrup in the sauce to control the level of spiciness and sweetness according to your taste.

III.   Veggie options: Feel free to incorporate other vegetables like bell peppers, radishes, or thinly sliced red cabbage to add more variety and nutrients to your poke bowl.

IV.   Protein alternatives: If desired, you can add plant-based protein sources like marinated tofu, tempeh, or chickpeas to boost the protein content of the bowl.

V.   Serving suggestions: Serve the vegan poke bowl as a wholesome and satisfying main course for lunch or dinner. It can be enjoyed as is or paired with a side of miso soup or a fresh green salad.

VI.   Meal prep: You can prepare the components of the vegan poke bowl in advance and assemble it just before serving. Keep the sauce, cooked rice, and steamed potatoes refrigerated separately until ready to use.

VII.   Savor the vibrant and nutritious flavors of this Vegan Poke Bowl. The combination of steamed potatoes, fresh vegetables, creamy avocado, and flavorful sauce creates a satisfying and wholesome plant-based meal. Whether you enjoy it as a light lunch or a hearty dinner, this colorful bowl is sure to delight your taste buds and nourish your body.

21. Coconut & Chili Pork Stir-Fry

Coconut & chili pork stir fry is a lovely mixture of pork, bok choy, spices and garnished with chili and coconut. It's a healthy and wholesome dinner for two. It's spicy, rich, and has delicious soft pork pieces.

Serve: 4

Prep Time: 20 minutes

List of Ingredients:

- 1 .5 tablespoons of ginger, grated
- 1/3 cup of coconut, shredded
- 15 oz of pork filet
- 2 bunches of baby bok choy
- 2 tablespoons of Chinese rice wine
- 1 tablespoon of soy sauce
- 2 tablespoons of oyster sauce
- Red chili, shredded for garnishing
- 1 teaspoon of chili paste
- 3 garlic cloves, crushed
- 1/3 cup of peanut oil
- 1/2 bunch of spring onions, chopped
- 6 oz of oyster mushrooms
- 10 oz of somen noodles, cooked

Method:

I. Prepare the marinade: In a bowl, combine minced garlic, grated ginger, chili paste, coconut milk, and oil. Set aside half of the mixture in a separate bowl. Add the pork to the remaining marinade and toss to coat. Cover and let it marinate for 15 minutes.

II. Heat oil in a pan: Heat oil in a large pan or wok over medium-high heat.

III. Stir-fry the pork: Remove the pork from the marinade, allowing any excess marinade to drip off, and add it to the hot pan. Stir-fry the pork until it is cooked through and nicely browned. Remove the pork from the pan and set it aside.

IV. Blanch the bok choy: Bring a pot of water to a boil and blanch the bok choy for about 3 minutes, until it is tender-crisp. Drain the bok choy and set it aside.

V. Heat oil in the wok: Heat oil in the same wok or pan over medium heat.

VI. Add spring onion and coconut mixture: Add the chopped spring onions and the reserved coconut mixture to the wok. Stir-fry for about 1 minute, until fragrant.

VII. Add mushrooms: Add the sliced mushrooms to the wok and continue stir-frying for about 2 minutes, until the mushrooms have softened.

VIII. Add wine, soy sauce, and oyster sauce: Pour in the wine, soy sauce, and oyster sauce. Stir well to combine.

IX. Return the pork to the wok: Add the cooked pork back into the wok and toss to coat it in the sauce. Continue cooking for about 3 minutes, allowing the flavors to meld together.

X. Serve with noodles: Serve the stir-fried pork over cooked noodles or rice, creating a bed for the dish.

XI. Garnish and serve: Garnish the dish with blanched bok choy, shredded red chili, and a sprinkle of coconut. Serve the Coconut and Chilli Pork Stir-Fry hot and enjoy!

Cooking Notes:

I. Adjusting spice level: You can adjust the amount of chili paste or add fresh chilies according to your desired level of spiciness.

II. Vegetable variations: Feel free to add other vegetables such as bell peppers, snap peas, or carrots for added color and texture.

III. Sauce consistency: If you prefer a thicker sauce, you can add a cornstarch slurry (mix cornstarch with a little water) to the sauce and cook until it thickens.

IV. Serving options: This stir-fry can be enjoyed on its own or served with steamed rice, noodles, or even alongside a bed of fresh salad greens.

V. Experiment with flavors: Feel free to experiment with additional seasonings such as lemongrass, lime juice, or cilantro to enhance the aromatic flavors of the dish.

VI. Indulge in the delightful flavors of this Coconut and Chilli Pork Stir-Fry. The combination of tender pork, aromatic spices, creamy coconut, and a touch of heat creates a mouthwatering dish that is perfect for a quick and satisfying meal. Enjoy the vibrant flavors and textures of this stir-fry, and customize it to your taste by adding your favorite vegetables or adjusting the spice level.

22. Ginger Scallion Sauce

Ginger scallion sauce is a 4-ingredient sauce, easy to make, glossy, and smother. It takes only 10 minutes to prepare and has an amazing aroma of ginger in it. After making it, let it sit for 20 minutes at least until the flavors are infused well in the oil.

Serve: 8

Prep Time: 10 minutes

List of Ingredients:

- 1 oz of ginger
- 1/4 cup of oil
- 10 stalks of scallions, chopped
- 1/2 teaspoon of salt

vvvvvvvvvvvvvvvvvvvvvvvvvvvv

Method:

I. Prepare the ingredients: Grate fresh ginger and finely chop scallions.

II. Combine the ingredients: In a bowl, add the grated ginger and chopped scallions.

III. Season with salt: Sprinkle a pinch of salt over the ginger and scallions.

IV. Heat the oil: In a small saucepan, heat oil until it is hot but not smoking.

V. Pour the hot oil: Carefully pour the hot oil over the ginger and scallions. Be cautious as the oil may splatter.

VI. Mix well: Stir the mixture well, ensuring that the hot oil coats the ginger and scallions evenly.

VII. Let it rest: Allow the ginger scallion sauce to sit for a few minutes, allowing the flavors to meld together.

VIII. Taste and adjust: Taste the sauce and adjust the seasoning according to your preference. You can add more salt or a splash of soy sauce for additional flavor.

IX. Serving options: Ginger scallion sauce is traditionally served as a condiment for various Asian dishes such as steamed chicken, poached fish, or noodles. It can also be used as a dipping sauce or drizzled over grilled meats or vegetables.

X. Storage: Store any leftover sauce in an airtight container in the refrigerator for up to one week.

XI.   Enjoy: Serve the Ginger Scallion Sauce with your favorite dishes and savor the aromatic and savory flavors it adds to your meal.

Cooking Notes:

I.   Freshness: For the best flavor, use freshly grated ginger and freshly chopped scallions.

II.   Adjusting heat: If you prefer a milder sauce, you can reduce the amount of grated ginger or use young ginger, which has a milder flavor.

III.   Customize the sauce: Feel free to personalize the sauce by adding additional ingredients such as minced garlic, sesame oil, or a dash of vinegar for extra tanginess.

IV.   Versatile condiment: Ginger scallion sauce pairs well with a wide range of dishes, so don't be afraid to experiment and explore different culinary combinations.

V.   Enjoy the vibrant and aromatic flavors of this homemade Ginger Scallion Sauce, a versatile condiment that adds a delightful zing to your favorite Asian-inspired dishes. With its fresh ginger, fragrant scallions, and a touch of heat from the hot oil, this sauce elevates the taste of your meals with its bold and savory profile. Drizzle it over your favorite proteins, use it as a dip, or incorporate it into stir-fries for a burst of flavor.

23. Hashima Dessert Soup

Hashima dessert soup is a delicious recipe and good for your skin. It keeps you youthful and is only made with 6 ingredients. It's an elegant and simple soup solution to enjoy during a whole day. It leaves you satisfied, refreshed, and cools you instantly after a long hectic day.

Serve: 10

Prep Time: 1 day 25 minutes

List of Ingredients:

- 7 oz of goji berries
- 1 oz of dried longan
- 8 oz of rock sugar
- 2 cups of water
- 5 oz of dried hashima
- 8 oz of red dates

vvvvvvvvvvvvvvvvvvvvvvvvvvvvvvvvv

Method:

I. Soak hashima: Place the hashima in a bowl and soak it overnight to soften and rehydrate the dried collagen.

II. Wash hashima: The next day, thoroughly rinse the soaked hashima under running water to remove any impurities or residue.

III. Prepare other ingredients: Rinse the dried longan and red dates to clean them. Then, bring them to a boil in a pot of water for about 2 minutes to soften them and release their flavors.

IV. Wash goji berries: Rinse the goji berries under running water to remove any dirt or debris.

V. Combine ingredients: Add the washed hashima to the pot with the boiled longan and red dates. Sprinkle in rock sugar (or other sweeteners of choice) to taste.

VI. Simmer the soup: Allow the soup to simmer gently over low heat for about 30 minutes, or until the hashima becomes translucent and tender.

VII. Adjust sweetness: Taste the soup and adjust the sweetness by adding more rock sugar if desired.

VIII. Serve hot or cold: Hashima dessert soup can be enjoyed either hot or chilled, depending on your preference. Serve it in bowls or small dessert cups.

IX. Garnish (optional): If desired, you can garnish the soup with a sprinkle of goji berries or additional dried fruits for added texture and visual appeal.

X. Storage: Any leftover hashima dessert soup can be stored in the refrigerator for up to 2 days. Reheat or consume it cold as desired.

XI. Enjoy: Savor the delicate and nourishing flavors of the hashima dessert soup as a sweet ending to a meal or as a soothing treat any time of the day.

Cooking Notes:

I. Soaking time: Hashima needs to be soaked overnight to soften properly. This allows it to absorb water and regain its gelatinous texture.

II. Sweetness: Adjust the sweetness of the soup by adding more or less rock sugar, depending on your taste preferences.

III. Additional ingredients: Feel free to enhance the soup by adding other ingredients like dried longan, red dates, lotus seeds, or even snow fungus to create variations of the traditional hashima dessert soup.

IV. Nutritional benefits: Hashima is believed to have various health benefits, including promoting skin health, nourishing the lungs, and improving overall vitality.

V. Indulge in the delicate and nourishing flavors of Hashima Dessert Soup. This traditional Chinese dessert features the rehydrated collagen known as hashima, combined with the natural sweetness of dried fruits. The soup is both comforting and refreshing, making it a delightful treat for any occasion. Whether enjoyed hot or chilled, this dessert soup offers a unique texture and a touch of sweetness that will surely satisfy your taste buds.

24. Jiaozi Chinese Pot stickers

Jiaozi Chinese Potstickers are low-carb dumplings that get ready in 40 minutes. These dumplings are easy to make with a delicious and smooth filling of scallions and arrowroot. A healthy, delicious pot sticker fried and crackling outside!

Serve: 3

Prep Time: 40 minutes

List of Ingredients:

- 3 bulbs of scallions, chopped
- 1 tablespoon of ginger, chopped
- ¼ teaspoon of coarse sea salt
- Avocado oil
- 20 oz of Daikon radish or turnip
- ⅛ teaspoon of ground white pepper
- 10 oz of ground chicken
- 1 teaspoon of sesame oil
- 1-2 teaspoons of arrowroot starch, omit for keto

Dumpling sauce

- 5 teaspoons of rice vinegar
- 5 tablespoons of coconut aminos
- ¼ teaspoon of sesame oil

Method:

I. Prepare the radish: Dice the tip of the radish and thinly slice it using a mandolin slicer.

II. Salt the radish slices: Place the radish slices on a sheet and sprinkle some salt over them. Let them sit aside for 15 minutes to draw out excess moisture.

III. Make the dumpling filling: In a bowl, combine all the ingredients for the filling, including the arrowroot starch and scallions. Mix until you have a sticky paste-like consistency. Place the filling in the refrigerator to firm up.

IV. Assemble the dumplings: Take a small amount of filling and place it in the center of a dumpling wrapper. Fold the wrapper in half, gently pressing the edges together to seal it. Fold and pleat the edges to create a half-moon shape.

V. Fry the dumplings: Heat oil in a skillet over medium heat. Place the dumplings in the skillet and fry them for about 2 minutes until the bottoms are golden brown. Cover the skillet with a lid and steam the dumplings for 3 minutes.

VI. Uncover and continue cooking: Remove the lid and cook the dumplings for another 50 seconds to crisp up the bottoms.

VII. Check for doneness: Check that the dumplings are cooked through by ensuring that the filling is hot and the wrappers are tender.

VIII. Serve hot: Remove the dumplings from the skillet and serve them hot with your choice of dipping sauce.

IX. Optional dipping sauce: Prepare a dipping sauce of your choice, such as soy sauce, vinegar, or a combination of both. You can also add ingredients like chili oil, sesame oil, or minced garlic to enhance the flavor.

X. Garnish (optional): If desired, garnish the pot stickers with some chopped scallions or sesame seeds for added visual appeal.

XI. Enjoy: Indulge in the delicious Jiaozi Chinese Pot Stickers, savoring the combination of the flavorful filling and crispy dumpling wrappers.

Cooking Notes:

I.   Wrappers: You can use store-bought dumpling wrappers or make your own from scratch.

II. Filling variations: Feel free to customize the filling by adding ingredients like minced pork, shrimp, cabbage, or other vegetables of your choice.

III. Freezing: If you have leftover uncooked dumplings, you can freeze them on a baking sheet and then transfer them to a freezer bag. Cook them directly from frozen when you're ready to enjoy them.

IV. Delight in the flavorful and satisfying Jiaozi Chinese Pot Stickers. These dumplings are a popular dish in Chinese cuisine, loved for their crispy bottoms and juicy fillings. Whether served as an appetizer, snack, or part of a larger meal, they are sure to impress your taste buds. Get creative with the fillings and dipping sauces to create a personalized culinary experience. Enjoy the process of making these pot stickers and share them with family and friends for a delightful dining experience.

25. Coconut Rice Cake

Coconut rice cake is made with coconut milk and rice flour. These cakes are perfect with coffee or tea to enjoy. The best snack party for your morning or evening with your loved ones around you. These cakes are a true resemblance of elegant and tasteful snacks.

Serve: 12

Prep Time: 30 minutes

List of Ingredients:

- 2 tablespoons of baking powder
- 2 cups of rice flour
- 1 pinch of salt
- 1 1/4 cups of granulated sugar
- 5 ounces of coconut milk
- 1 teaspoon of vanilla
- 4 eggs
- 2 tablespoons of butter, melted

vvvvvvvvvvvvvvvvvvvvvvvvvvvv

Method:

I. Preheat the oven: Preheat your oven to 375°F (190°C).

II. Prepare the dry ingredients: In a bowl, combine the rice flour, baking powder, and salt together. Mix well to ensure an even distribution of the ingredients.

III. Prepare the wet ingredients: In another large bowl, beat the eggs, sugar, coconut milk, melted butter, and vanilla extract together. Mix until well combined and the sugar has dissolved.

IV. Combine the batter: Gradually add the flour mixture to the wet ingredients. Stir well to form a smooth batter. Ensure there are no lumps in the mixture.

V. Divide the batter: Divide the batter evenly into individual cake tins or a single cake pan, depending on your preference.

VI. Bake in the oven: Place the cake tins or pan in the preheated oven and bake for approximately 20 minutes, or until a toothpick inserted into the center of the cake comes out clean.

VII.   Remove from the oven: Carefully remove the cake from the oven using oven mitts or heat-resistant gloves.

VIII.   Allow to cool: Let the cake cool in the tins or pan for about 10 minutes. This will make it easier to remove the cake from the tins or cut it into slices.

IX.   Slice and serve: If you used individual cake tins, gently remove the cakes from the tins. Alternatively, if you used a single cake pan, cut the cake into desired slices.

X.   Optional garnish: You can dust the coconut rice cake with powdered sugar or sprinkle shredded coconut on top for added texture and presentation.

XI.   Enjoy: Serve the coconut rice cake as a delightful dessert or snack. It pairs well with a cup of tea or coffee.

Cooking Notes:

I.   Rice flour: Ensure that you are using rice flour specifically meant for baking, as other types of rice flour may have different textures and properties.

II.   Coconut milk: Use full-fat coconut milk for a rich and creamy flavor. Shake the can before opening it to ensure that the coconut cream and water are well combined.

III.   Variations: For added flavor, you can incorporate ingredients such as lemon zest, orange zest, or shredded coconut into the batter.

IV.   Storage: Once cooled, store any leftover coconut rice cake in an airtight container at room temperature for up to 2 days, or in the refrigerator for longer shelf life.

V.   Enjoy the delightful Coconut Rice Cake, which combines the aromatic flavors of coconut and the soft texture of rice flour. This versatile treat can be enjoyed on its own or served with a scoop of ice cream or a drizzle of caramel sauce for extra indulgence. Experiment with different variations and toppings to make it your own.

26. Yum Yum Sauce

Yum yum, the sauce is a favorite Japanese sauce that gets ready in just 5 minutes. It's only a 4-ingredient sauce that anybody can make at home. It is used as a spread over fish or chicken. It's spicy, creamy, and tasteful.

Serve: 2 cups

Prep Time: 5 minutes

List of Ingredients:

- 6 tablespoons of sweet chili sauce
- 6 teaspoons of hot sauce
- 1 cup of mayonnaise
- 4 tablespoons of honey

vvvvvvvvvvvvvvvvvvvvvvvvvvvvvv

Method:

I. Prepare the sauce: In a Mason jar or mixing bowl, combine 6 tablespoons of sweet chili sauce, 6 teaspoons of hot sauce, 1 cup of mayonnaise, and 4 tablespoons of honey. Mix well to ensure all ingredients are thoroughly combined.

II. Refrigerate the sauce: Cover the jar or bowl with a lid or plastic wrap, and place it in the refrigerator. Allowing the sauce to chill will enhance the flavors and help meld the ingredients together.

III. Let the flavors develop: Allow the Yum Yum sauce to sit in the refrigerator for at least 1 hour or overnight. This will give the flavors time to develop and create a harmonious taste.

IV. Serve and enjoy: Once chilled and the flavors have melded, the Yum Yum sauce is ready to be served. Use it as a dipping sauce for sushi, seafood, vegetables, or as a flavorful accompaniment to grilled meats or stir-fried dishes.

Cooking Notes:

I.   Sweet chili sauce: Look for commercially available sweet chili sauce in the Asian section of your grocery store. You can adjust the amount of sweet chili sauce used based on your desired level of spiciness.

II. Hot sauce: Use your preferred hot sauce, such as sriracha or Tabasco, to add a bit of heat to the sauce. Adjust the amount to suit your taste.

III. Mayonnaise: Opt for a good-quality mayonnaise for the best taste and texture of the Yum Yum sauce.

IV. Flavor variations: You can personalize the Yum Yum sauce by adding additional ingredients such as garlic powder, paprika, or a squeeze of lime juice for a tangy twist.

V.   Storage: Store any leftover Yum Yum sauce in an airtight container in the refrigerator for up to one week. Make sure to give it a good stir before using it again, as separation may occur.

VI. Enjoy the creamy and tangy Yum Yum Sauce as a versatile condiment that adds a burst of flavor to your favorite dishes. Experiment with different ingredient ratios to customize the sauce to your taste preferences.

27. Persian Salad Shirazi

Persian Salad Shirazi is a wonderful salad with lots of flavors of vegetables and spices packed in the bowl. It's healthy, crunchy, and gets ready in just 20 minutes. Full nutrients packed meal for the family.

Serve: 4

Prep Time: 20 minutes

List of Ingredients:

- 1 red onion, diced
- Lemon, juiced
- 1 teaspoon of dried dill
- Salt and pepper, to taste
- 4 ripe tomatoes, diced
- 2 cucumbers, diced
- 3 tablespoons of olive oil
- 1 tablespoon of dried mint
- 1 teaspoon of ground sumac

vvvvvvvvvvvvvvvvvvvvvvvvvvvvvv

Method:

I. Prepare the salad: In a bowl, combine tomatoes, red onion, cucumbers, mint, dill, sumac, salt, and pepper. These ingredients give the salad its fresh and vibrant flavors.

II. Add the dressing: Squeeze lime juice over the salad and drizzle with olive oil. The lime juice adds a tangy brightness, while the olive oil brings a rich and smooth element to the dish.

III. Toss the ingredients: Using a salad spoon or tongs, toss the ingredients together gently but thoroughly. This ensures that the flavors are evenly distributed and the salad is well coated with the dressing.

IV. Serve and enjoy: Transfer the Persian Salad Shirazi to a serving dish or individual plates. It is best served chilled and can be enjoyed as a refreshing side dish or a light meal on its own.

Cooking Notes:

I. Tomatoes: Choose ripe and juicy tomatoes for the best flavor. You can use a combination of different types, such as cherry tomatoes or heirloom tomatoes, to add variety to the salad.

II. Red onion: Slice the red onion thinly to provide a mild and slightly sweet onion flavor without overpowering the other ingredients.

III. Cucumbers: Use fresh and crisp cucumbers. If the cucumbers have thick skin, you can peel them before adding to the salad.

IV. Fresh herbs: Finely chop the mint and dill to release their aromatic flavors and add a pleasant herbaceous note to the salad.

V. Sumac: Sumac is a tangy and slightly lemony spice commonly used in Middle Eastern cuisine. It adds a unique citrusy flavor to the salad.

VI. Seasoning: Adjust the amount of salt, pepper, and sumac according to your taste preferences.

VII. Serving suggestions: Persian Salad Shirazi pairs well with grilled meats, kebabs, or as a refreshing accompaniment to a mezze platter.

VIII. Storage: It is best to consume the salad immediately for maximum freshness. However, if you have leftovers, store them in an airtight container in the refrigerator for up to 1-2 days.

IX. Enjoy the vibrant flavors and crisp textures of Persian Salad Shirazi, a classic Iranian salad that is simple to prepare and bursting with refreshing goodness.

28. Mongolian Beef & Noodle

Mongolian beef & noodle is a delicious pan-Asian recipe. It has tender rice noodles and sweet and spicy flavors of sauces. The seasoning makes it a special dish for dinner. It's a restaurant-style beef & noodle dish that tastes amazing. Delicious noodles, mouth-watering beef, and sauces make it a tasty meal for tonight.

Serve: 6

Prep Time: 30 minutes

List of Ingredients:

- 16 oz of ground beef
- 1 tablespoon of sesame oil
- 2 teaspoons of garlic paste
- ¼ cup of hoisin sauce
- ½ cup of soy sauce
- 1 cup of beef broth
- 1 tablespoon of sesame seeds
- 8 oz of rice noodles
- 2 tablespoons of cornstarch
- 5 tablespoons of ginger paste
- 1 teaspoon of chili paste
- ¼ cup of brown sugar
- ½ teaspoon of red pepper flakes
- 1 green onion, sliced

vvvvvvvvvvvvvvvvvvvvvvvvvvvvvv

Method:

I. Cook the noodles: Prepare the noodles according to the package instructions. Drain the water and set aside.

II. Heat the skillet: Heat oil in a large skillet or wok over medium-high heat.

III. Cook the ground beef: Add the ground beef to the skillet and cook until it is no longer pink, breaking it up into smaller pieces as it cooks.

IV. Add garlic-ginger paste: Stir in the garlic-ginger paste and cook for an additional minute to infuse the flavors.

V. Prepare the sauce: In a bowl, combine brown sugar, soy sauce, hoisin sauce, chili paste, and beef broth. Whisk well to ensure the ingredients are thoroughly combined.

VI. Add the sauce: Pour the sauce mixture into the skillet with the cooked beef. Stir well to coat the beef evenly.

VII. Thicken the sauce: In a separate bowl, mix cornstarch with water to create a slurry. Add the slurry to the skillet and stir continuously until the sauce thickens.

VIII. Add green onions: Incorporate 1/4 cup of chopped green onions into the skillet. These will add a fresh and onion flavor to the dish.

IX. Adjust seasonings: Taste the sauce and adjust the seasonings to your preference. You can add more soy sauce, brown sugar, or chili paste to suit your taste.

X. Sauté for 2 minutes: Continue cooking the beef and sauce for an additional 2 minutes, allowing the flavors to meld together.

XI. Add cooked noodles: Add the cooked noodles to the skillet, tossing them with the beef and sauce until they are well coated.

XII. Garnish and serve: Garnish the Mongolian beef and noodles with additional chopped green onions and sesame seeds for added flavor and visual appeal. Serve hot.

Cooking Notes:

I. Noodles: You can use your choice of noodles, such as egg noodles or rice noodles, depending on your preference.

II. Ground beef: Choose lean ground beef for a healthier option, or use ground chicken or turkey as a substitute.

III. Garlic-ginger paste: You can make a paste by combining minced garlic and grated ginger in equal amounts or use pre-made paste available at grocery stores.

IV. Adjust the heat: If you prefer a spicier dish, you can increase the amount of chili paste or add red pepper flakes.

V. Vegetables: Feel free to add vegetables like bell peppers, carrots, or broccoli to the stir-fry for extra color and nutrition.

VI. Customization: Mongolian beef is versatile, and you can personalize it by incorporating your favorite ingredients or sauces.

VII. Serving suggestion: Serve the Mongolian beef and noodles as a complete meal or pair it with steamed vegetables or a side salad.

VIII. Enjoy the flavorful combination of tender beef, savory sauce, and noodles in this Mongolian Beef and Noodle dish. It's a satisfying and delicious meal that can be easily prepared at home.

29. Spicy Baked Tofu

Spicy baked tofu is a healthy, protein-packed dish with lots of delicious flavors. Here the tofu is marinated with soy sauce, chili sauce, hoisin sauce, and garlic and is baked in the oven. If you want to be more creative with your tofu, then grill it for an amazing taste & texture.

Serve: 4

Prep Time: 1 hour 45 minutes

List of Ingredients:

- 12 oz of tofu
- 2 tablespoons of Japanese soy sauce
- 2 tablespoons of ginger, minced
- Cooking spray
- 2 tablespoons of Asian chili sauce
- 5 tablespoons of Hoisin sauce

wwwwwwwwwwwwwwwwwwwwwwwww

Method:

I. Prepare the tofu: Remove the tofu from its packaging and gently press it between paper towels or kitchen towels to remove excess water. Let it sit for 5 minutes to remove any remaining moisture.

II. Cut the tofu: Cut the tofu into half-inch thick strips. This will ensure that the tofu cooks evenly and absorbs the flavors of the marinade.

III. Prepare the marinade: In a plastic bag, combine soy sauce, ginger, chili sauce, and hoisin sauce. Close the bag and mix the ingredients well to create a flavorful marinade.

IV. Marinate the tofu: Place the tofu strips in the plastic bag with the marinade. Seal the bag and gently shake it to coat the tofu evenly. Place the bag in the refrigerator and let the tofu marinate for at least 1 hour. This allows the tofu to absorb the flavors of the marinade.

V. Preheat the oven: Preheat your oven to 375°F (190°C). This temperature ensures that the tofu cooks thoroughly and develops a nice crispy texture.

VI. Prepare the baking sheet: Spray a baking sheet with cooking spray or line it with parchment paper to prevent the tofu from sticking.

VII.   Remove excess moisture: Take the marinated tofu out of the refrigerator and gently pat it dry with paper towels to remove any excess moisture. This step helps the tofu crisp up during baking.

VIII.   Arrange tofu on the baking sheet: Place the tofu strips in a single layer on the prepared baking sheet. Make sure they are not overlapping to ensure even cooking.

IX.   Bake the tofu: Put the baking sheet with the tofu in the preheated oven and bake for about 15 minutes. Keep an eye on the tofu to prevent it from burning. The baking time may vary depending on the thickness of the tofu slices and your desired level of crispiness.

X.   Check for doneness: After 15 minutes, check the tofu for doneness. It should have a golden brown color and a crispy texture on the outside.

XI.   Remove from the oven: Once the tofu is baked to your desired crispiness, remove the baking sheet from the oven and let the tofu cool slightly before serving.

XII.   Serve and enjoy: Serve the spicy baked tofu as a protein-rich main dish or use it as a flavorful addition to salads, stir-fries, or rice bowls.

Cooking Notes:

I.   Tofu pressing: Pressing the tofu helps remove excess moisture, allowing it to absorb flavors better and achieve a crispier texture during baking.

II.   Marinade options: Feel free to adjust the marinade ingredients to suit your taste preferences. You can add or reduce the amount of ginger, chili sauce, or hoisin sauce.

III.   Baking time: The baking time may vary depending on the thickness of the tofu slices and your oven's heat distribution. Keep an eye on the tofu to avoid overcooking or burning.

IV.   Serving suggestions: Enjoy the spicy baked tofu on its own as a flavorful protein option, or use it in wraps, sandwiches, or Buddha bowls. It pairs well with steamed rice, quinoa, or noodles.

V.   Storage: Leftover tofu can be stored in the refrigerator for a few days. Reheat it in the oven or microwave before serving.

VI.   Indulge in the spicy and savory flavors of this baked tofu recipe. The crispy exterior and tender interior make it a delicious and versatile protein option for various dishes.

30. Almond Butter Sauce

Almond butter sauce is a perfect Asian sauce to pair with dishes. It's a vegan, gluten-free versatile sauce best to enjoy with a noodle bowl, tofu marinade, or even for spring rolls. It's a spicy and creamy sauce that has a rich taste and texture.

Serve: 4-6

Prep Time: 5 minutes

List of Ingredients:

- ⅓ cup of almond butter
- 1 tablespoon of sesame oil
- 1 tablespoon of tamari
- 2 tablespoons of maple syrup
- 1 clove of garlic, minced
- 3 tablespoons of water
- ¼ teaspoon of red pepper flakes
- 2 tablespoons of lemon juice
- ½ teaspoon of ginger, minced

vvvvvvvvvvvvvvvvvvvvvvvvvvvvvvv

Method:

I. Roast the almonds: Preheat your oven to 350°F (175°C). Spread the almonds on a baking sheet and roast them for about 10 minutes, or until they turn golden brown and fragrant. Keep an eye on them to prevent burning.

II. Cool and blend: Allow the roasted almonds to cool completely. Once cooled, transfer them to a blender or food processor. Blend until you achieve a smooth and creamy almond butter consistency. This may take a few minutes, depending on the power of your blender or food processor.

III. Heat the saucepan: Heat a saucepan over medium heat and add oil. Heat the oil until it becomes hot but not smoking.

IV. Add mustard seeds: Add the mustard seeds to the hot oil. Allow them to crackle and pop, which should take about 30 seconds.

V.   Add spices: Stir in the asafetida, turmeric powder, green chilies, and roasted fenugreek powder. Sauté the spices for 30-40 seconds, stirring constantly to prevent burning.

VI.   Turn off the heat: Once the spices have released their aroma and are well combined, turn off the heat and remove the saucepan from the stove.

VII.   Mix with almond butter: Transfer the sautéed spices to the blender or food processor with the almond butter. Blend the mixture until the spices are fully incorporated and the sauce is smooth and well combined.

VIII.   Season with salt: Taste the almond butter sauce and season it with salt according to your preference. Add salt gradually, tasting as you go, until you reach the desired flavor.

IX.   Adjust consistency: If the almond butter sauce is too thick, you can add a small amount of warm water or vegetable broth to thin it out. Add a little at a time until you achieve the desired consistency. Stir well to combine.

X.   Heat and serve: If desired, heat the almond butter sauce gently in a saucepan before serving. This will help enhance the flavors and make the sauce more pourable. Be careful not to overheat or boil the sauce.

XI.   Serve and enjoy: Almond butter sauce is now ready to be served. It can be used as a dip, drizzled over roasted vegetables or grilled meats, or incorporated into various recipes for added flavor and creaminess.

Cooking Notes:

I.   Storage: Store the almond butter sauce in an airtight container in the refrigerator. It should keep well for up to two weeks. Before using, allow the sauce to come to room temperature or gently warm it before serving.

II.   Customization: Feel free to adjust the spices and seasonings in the almond butter sauce according to your taste preferences. You can add more or less fenugreek powder, mustard seeds, or green chilies to suit your desired level of heat and flavor.

III.   Texture: The consistency of the almond butter sauce can be adjusted by adding more or less water or vegetable broth. Start with a smaller amount and gradually add more until you achieve the desired thickness.

IV.   Versatility: Almond butter sauce can be used in a variety of dishes, such as curries, stir-fries, salad dressings, or as a dipping sauce for vegetables or grilled tofu. It adds a creamy and nutty flavor to your culinary creations.

V.   Nut allergy: If you or someone you're serving has a nut allergy, consider substituting the almond butter with sunflower seed butter or another nut-free alternative.

VI.   Enjoy the rich and nutty flavors of this homemade almond butter sauce. Its versatility makes it a delightful addition to various dishes, providing a creamy and flavorful experience.

Author's Afterthoughts

thank you

Being a single mother never quite gets "easy", but it's an especially entertaining and complicated feat when they're young. My kiddos are like bouncy balls that have been charged with endless energy. They're here, they're there, they're everywhere! While I have gotten used to all of our adventures, I definitely have to take a moment to thank you for supporting my work.

Not only does it allow me to spend more time with my kids, but it also helps me pay the bills and continue funding new cookbook projects as a single mom. Cooking for my kids during their picky eating phases is always tricky, but thankfully I have you to support me so I can get creative in the kitchen and solve their cravings and your life with all of my recipes.

Just hang in there because it's only a matter of time before my next book comes out, but until then, I'd really like it if you could share your thoughts about my recipes with me. Also, what kind of recipes would you like to see more of? School lunches? Meals for certain allergies? Whatever you come up with will benefit all the moms out there (including myself) who struggle to think of delicious healthy meals our kids will actually eat.

Keep me posted!

Josephine Ellis.